A Child's View of Grief

The Educational Resource Library Asks that you please return your library materials when you are done with them. If they have been helpful to you, they will help another. If you would like to purchase this title, please contact the librarian and she can assist you with your purchase.
This Library copy is not for sale.

 Vail Valley Medical Center

Also by Alan Wolfelt

Healing A Child's Grieving Heart
100 Practical Ideas for Families, Friends, and Caregivers

Healing A Teen's Grieving Heart
100 Practical Ideas for Families, Friends, and Caregivers

Healing The Bereaved Child
Grief Gardening, Growth Through Grief, and Other
Touchstones for Caregivers

Healing Your Grieving Heart for Kids
100 Practical Ideas

Healing Your Grieving Heart for Teens
100 Practical Ideas

How I Feel
A Coloring Book for Grieving Children

Understanding Your Grief
Ten Essential Touchstones for Finding Hope
and Healing Your Heart

When Your Pet Dies
A Guide to Mourning, Remembering, and Healing

A Child's View of Grief

A Guide for Parents, Teachers, and Counselors

Alan D. Wolfelt, Ph.D.

Companion
PRESS

Fort Collins, Colorado
An imprint of the Center for Loss and Life Transition

Companion Press is an imprint of the Center for Loss and Life Transition, 3735 Broken Bow Road, Fort Collins, Colorado 80526, (970) 226-6050.
www.centerforloss.com

Companion Press books may be purchased in bulk for sales promotions, premiums or fundraisers. Please contact the publisher at the above address for more information.

Printed in the United States of America

13 12 11 10 09 08 07 06 05 04   5 4 3 2 1

ISBN 1-879651-43-2

Contents

Preface

A Child's View of Grief is a practical guide for adults who
want to help grieving children. Perhaps no greater helping
opportunity exists than helping a child whose life has been
touched by the death of someone loved.

Without a doubt, communicating with children about death is
one of the most challenging experiences adults ever face. It is
also one of the most important.

A Child's View of Grief explores a variety of important topics
related to children and grief. This guide will help caring adults
increase their understanding of how to talk with children
about death and grief. There are special sections on involving
children in the funeral and adolescent mourning.

Introduction

When someone loved dies, children grieve. The most important factor in how children react to the death is the response of the adults in their lives. Caring adults—whether they are parents, relatives, or friends—can help children during this tragic time. Handled with warmth and understanding, a child's early experiences with death can be opportunities to learn about life and living as well as death and dying.

For parents and other adult caregivers, the first step in learning how to help children deal with death is to become educated about grief. Well-intentioned adults sometimes pass on their own anxieties and fears to the children they are trying to help. Studies show that children often suffer more from the loss of parental support during this time than from the death itself.

Children in our society are referred to as the "forgotten mourners." Children grieve, but all too often they don't get the opportunity to express their feelings openly. This is a situation concerned adults must address. The challenge is to learn how to establish "helping-healing" relationships with children whose lives have been touched by the death of someone loved. When caring adults meet this challenge, children are capable of reconciling grief in healthy ways.

Children & Death: An Historical Perspective

In early America, death was a familiar experience. When several generations of a family lived in the same household, children were surrounded by aging, illness, and death. They watched grandparents grow old. They gathered with other family members when death occurred. Usually funerals were held in the home.

Under these circumstances, children realized a significant loss had occurred. Along with their parents and siblings, they experienced tears and sorrow. Death was something that happened all around them. As a result, they came to know it gradually. For children in early America, death was not a mystery.

Today, children live in a "grief-avoiding" culture. For a variety of reasons, children in the United States often grow up without being exposed to the pain of grief during childhood. Modern medicine, for example, has drastically reduced infant and child mortality and has prolonged life expectancy for the aged.

Families are now also geographically scattered. Deaths occur thousands of miles from home. Even if different generations remain in the same area, the increased use of hospitals and nursing homes reduces the chances that children will witness the aging and dying of their loved ones. Consequently, many children do not have the opportunity to experience the normal grief that accompanies these events.

Ironically, children today are continually confronted by situations where they see that life no longer exists. They find a dead bird in the yard. Their pet dog is hit by a car or they watch TV and see the results of an earthquake or airplane crash. The questions they ask about death grow out of these experiences of daily living. They turn to the adults closest to them for help in understanding difficult questions about death, such as "Will my parents die?" and "What happens to people after they die?"

Parents need to answer these questions openly and in language that children can understand. Being sensitive to a child's needs can make a critical difference in whether the child's first experiences with death are a helpful or harmful part of their emotional growth. If children are not given honest answers appropriate to their age levels, they often develop distorted attitudes concerning death, dying, and funerals. These attitudes, unfortunately, may stay with them for the rest of their lives.

Children Teach Adults About Grief

Children respond to the death of someone loved in different ways. Each child's response is unique. Rather than prescribing what their grief experiences should be, parents and other caring adults must allow children to be the teachers. Given the opportunity, they will share with adults their personal journeys through grief. Grieving children have so much wisdom to offer. Adults need only learn how to listen.

Adults should never assume they know exactly how children feel when someone loved has died—or that individual children in a certain age group will understand death in the same way. Nor should they determine for children when it's time to stop grieving. Instead, children can teach adults what the experience is uniquely like for them.

Caring adults need to communicate several important attitudes: respect, acceptance, warmth, and understanding. Respect means treating children as separate persons without being possessive or purposely damaging their self-esteem. Acceptance involves supporting them without judging their behavior. Rather than approval or disapproval, acceptance means recognizing that children are unique and need to be acknowledged for themselves.

Another important attitude in a helping-healing relationship is warmth—a demonstration of personal closeness to grieving children. Adults need to remember that two-thirds of all communication is non-verbal. Behavior always speaks louder than words. Tone of voice, eye contact, posture, and facial gestures are a few of the non-verbal cues adults can use to help children teach them about grief. For adults, understanding or being aware of their own experiences with loss might affect their capacity to be emotionally available to grieving children. Adults who are able to separate their own needs from the needs of the children they wish to help make better students. These adults are more able to learn what grieving children have to teach.

With these attitudes, adults can work with children through individual grief experiences, lending a supportive, stabilizing presence.

The Importance of Empathy

When someone dies, adults need to create safe environments where children can openly express their grief. To do so, adults must convey empathy and have the courage to become actively involved in the emotional suffering that is a normal part of grief. Empathy means being able to recognize a child's inner feelings—from the child's point of view.

Adults convey empathy when grieving children feel understood and supported. To let children know their feelings are understood helps them feel secure, trusted, warm, and affirmed. Empathy is the essence of a helping-healing relationship.

The ability of adults to communicate empathy has multiple benefits for children whose lives have been touched by death:

• They are more likely to share deep and personal feelings.
• They feel secure in a trusting environment where they don't feel the need for self-protection or isolation.
• They are able to explore puzzling feelings and grow toward self-understanding and reconciliation of their grief.

While parents may have considerable knowledge about grief, without empathy a helping-healing relationship cannot occur. It is the foundation upon which all other helping qualities are built.

How a Grieving Child Feels

When someone loved dies, children express themselves in a variety of ways. Caring adults need to be aware of these forms of expression and recognize them as natural ways children work through their grief. Twelve dimensions of grief commonly experienced by grieving children are listed below. This list is not all-inclusive nor mutually exclusive. These grief responses occur in no specific order of progression. Each child's responses are uniquely different.

<u>Dimensions of Childhood Grief</u>

Apparent lack of feelings

Acting-out behavior

Physiological changes

Fear

Regressive behavior

Guilt and self-blame

"Big-Man" or "Big-Woman" syndrome

Relief

Disorganization and panic

Loss and loneliness

Explosive emotions

Reconciliation

Apparent lack of feelings

Children often respond to the death of someone loved with emotional shock and an apparent lack of feelings. They can be playing in the yard only hours or even minutes after learning of the death. Rather than being inappropriate, this behavior is a protective mechanism and nature's way of caring for children. It allows them to detach themselves from the pain in the only way they can.

Adults are often confused by this apparent indifference. However, they should recognize it as a child's way of naturally pushing away, at least temporarily, the knowledge that a loved one has died. Adults at this time must be supportive and accept this behavior as a necessary step toward healing.

Adults can provide opportunities for children to mourn in healthy ways, but should never force them to feel something before they are ready for the pain that precedes healing. Just as an adult puts a Band-Aid on a child's physical wound, adults must respect a child's need to temporarily cover up emotional wounds.

Regressive behavior

Under the normal stress of grief, children often return to a sense of protection and security they experienced at earlier times in their lives. This need is manifested in different ways:

a desire to be rocked or nursed; difficulty in being separated from parents; or requests for parents to do simple tasks, such as tying shoes, that children could previously do for themselves. They may also have difficulty in working independently at school. During this time, a child might also need constant individual attention, be suddenly afraid of the dark, or talk "baby talk." Regressive behaviors in bereaved children are usually temporary. If children are allowed the freedom to return to simpler, safer times, they will usually emerge from their mourning more competent. Children who are not allowed to regress, however, sometimes bury the pain within themselves.

Regression can happen at any time in the grief experience, but it usually occurs immediately following the death. The efforts of parents and other adults at this time should include providing children a supportive presence that permits them to share their conflicting thoughts and feelings without fear of judgment.

"Big-Man" or "Big-Woman" syndrome

The opposite of regressive behavior among grieving children is the "Big-Man" or "Big-Woman" syndrome. This is apparent when a child attempts to grow up quickly and exhibits adult behavior in an effort to replace the person who has died. This forced maturity can be the result of simply carrying out the instructions of respected adults: "You'll now have to be the man (or woman) of the house."

Although well-intentioned, adults who deliver this message are unaware of its potentially damaging impact. Sometimes a child unconsciously adopts this syndrome as a symbolic means of trying to keep the one who has died alive. By filling the loved one's role, a child doesn't have to acknowledge the full effect of the loss on his or her life. "Big-Man" or "Big-Woman" behavior in children is sometimes reinforced by grieving adults who find it easier to respond to children at this inappropriate level. In its extreme form, a child literally serves as a replacement for a dead spouse. When this occurs, self-identity and self-esteem are often severely damaged.

Adults can take a major step toward preventing forced maturity in grieving children. They can do this by preventing other adults from handing out such trite advice as "You'll have to take care of your mother now that your dad is gone." This kind of comment only results in the development of frustrated or depressed children who are not allowed to grieve in ways appropriate to their ages.

Explosive emotions

This dimension of grief is often the most upsetting for adults. Parents and others are uncertain how to respond to expressions of complex emotions such as anger, blame, hatred, terror, resentment, rage and jealousy.

Behind these explosive emotions, however, are a child's more primary feelings of pain, helplessness, frustration, fear, and hurt caused by the death of someone loved. Anger and other related emotions are natural, intelligent responses by a child in an effort to restore the valued relationship that has been lost.

A child's anger and rage may be directed toward anyone: the surviving parent, a teacher, friends, God, or the world in general. The fact that the dead person does not come back, despite the explosive emotions, is part of the reality-testing children need for the eventual healing process. Although confusing for adults, a child's ability to show explosive emotions is healthy. It provides a means of temporarily protesting the painful reality of the loss. Children who either do not give themselves permission to protest, or don't receive permission from others, may turn their anger inward. The result is often low self-esteem, depression, chronic feelings of guilt, and physical complaints.

The major role of the caring adult during periods of explosive emotions is to be a supportive stabilizer. Be understanding. Encourage and validate these emotions without judging, retaliating, or arguing. Allow children to let go of pent-up emotions. Healthy grief requires that we express, not repress, these feelings in a safe and loving environment.

Acting-out behavior

Many children will express the pain of grief through acting-out behavior. After experiencing the death of someone loved, children may have temper outbursts, become unusually loud, initiate fights, defy authority, or simply rebel against everyone. Sometimes grades will drop, or the child will assume a general I-don't-care attitude. Older children may talk about running away from home. For adults, understanding and appropriately responding to this acting-out behavior is often difficult. To establish a helping-healing relationship with children who are demonstrating this dimension of grief, adults need to first examine what causes it. Some of the factors that influence acting-out in grieving children are:

Feelings of insecurity. Grieving children naturally experience a sense of insecurity following the death of someone loved. In contrast, acted-out feelings unconsciously provide them with a sense of strength, control, and power.

Feeling of abandonment. When someone loved dies, children sometimes feel that the person has abandoned them. Consequently, they feel unloved; their self-esteem may be low. Acting-out behavior creates a self-fulfilling prophecy: "See, nobody loves me."

A desire to provoke punishment. Unconsciously, grieving children may feel so guilty when someone loved dies that they want to be punished for the death. Acting-out behavior elicits

16

that punishment. The acting-out behavior may even be directed toward trying to get the person who died to come back. The rationale: "If I'm bad, Dad will have to come back and make me behave."

A desire to externalize feelings of grief. Acting-out behavior is often demonstrated in children who have been grieving within themselves but not sharing this grief outwardly. Some adults mistakenly assume that children are too young to need to talk out thoughts and feelings about grief. The result is that many children grieve but do not mourn. Acting-out is, consequently, a way of saying, "I hurt, too."

For parents and other adults, the key to responding to acting-out behavior is to allow children to teach us what their needs are. By doing so, adults can help children heal the wounds resulting from the death.

Loss and loneliness

This dimension, feelings of loss and loneliness, is often the most difficult for grieving children. It never takes place all at once and may continue for months or years after the death. Usually, these feelings begin when a child finally realizes that the person who has died is never coming back.

As children struggle to come to terms with the finality of the death, they may become depressed. This condition is a natural response to their loss. During this time, children may demonstrate a lack of interest in themselves or others, a change in appetite and sleeping patterns, nervousness, an inability to enjoy life, and low self-esteem. Children are particularly vulnerable at this time. They may become extremely dependent on others and sometimes on someone who reminds them of the person who has died. Caring adults play an important role in helping children grow through this dimension of grief. By communicating in both words and touch, adults can assure children they are not alone in their grief and help them move toward encountering life, living, and loving once again.

Reconciliation: the final dimension

Reconciliation is the final dimension of healthy grief. While children never get over their grief, they become reconciled to it. At this point, children recognize life will be different without the presence of the person who died, yet they have a renewed sense of energy and confidence and want to become involved in the activities of life once again.

Adults should never prescribe specific timetables to reach reconciliation. A child will proceed at his or her own pace, depending on age, personality, social environment, and relationship to the person who has died. Changes often noted during a child's reconciliation process include:

- A return to stable eating and sleeping patterns
- A renewed sense of well-being
- A subjective sense of release from the person who has died
- An increase in thinking and judgment capabilities
- An increased ability to enjoy life's experiences
- A recognition of the finality of the death
- An establishment of new and healthy relationships

Perhaps the most important gain in the reconciliation process is the child's ability to successfully cope with the loss. The child has come to terms with grief and is ready to get on with the business of living. And while the sense of loss may reoccur, it's softer; the pangs of grief will be less frequent and less severe.

Even when children reach reconciliation, "griefbursts" may occur on and off for years. A griefburst is a sudden, sharp feeling of grief and loss that seems to come out of nowhere. During a griefburst, a child may feel an overwhelming sense of missing the person who has died. He may cry or sob and feel anxious. Griefbursts are normal and natural and are sometimes triggered by a specific holiday or event that reminds them of the person who has died.

Reconciliation can best be achieved with the assistance of helping-healing adults who allow children to move toward their grief, not away from it. Children need to know that grief is nothing to be ashamed of.

The Six Reconciliation Needs of Mourning

How does a grieving child mourn his way from the starting point of his grief through his many thoughts and feelings to the destination of reconciliation and growth? Asked more simply, how does the grieving child heal?

I believe the grieving child heals, over time, when her mourning needs are consistently met. This section defines what I term "the six reconciliation needs of mourning." Others have labeled these the tasks of childhood mourning.

Need 1. Acknowledge the reality of the death.

Before he can move on in his grief journey, the grieving child must be helped to gently confront the reality that someone he loves has died and will not return.

Of course, children must be provided with an open and honest explanation (at their level of developmental understanding) about the nature and cause of the death if they are to meet this mourning need. As caring adults, we must openly share clear information about the death with the affected children. Remember, kids can cope with what they know. They cannot cope with what they don't know.

We as a society must work to overcome our instinct to protect children from sad news. We must also refrain from thinking that children are "too young to understand." Perhaps they are too young to fully understand everything about the death, but they are never too young to feel.

The news of a death is best conveyed by someone close to the child. When possible, it shouldn't come from someone who doesn't have a pre-existing, stabilizing relationship with the child. Keep in mind the importance of eye contact, a comforting tone of voice and appropriate physical comfort that conveys security. Be certain to avoid euphemisms such as "sleep" and "passed away" that will only confuse the child.

If a child teaches you that she doesn't understand what death is all about, explain that the dead person's body has stopped working and it will never again work the way it used to. The person's body will not see or hear and won't talk, move or breathe anymore. The body won't feel cold or hot or be happy or sad. When a person's body dies, the person doesn't feel anything anymore. These kinds of explanations help the child understand that the person who died cannot come back. Being supportive of the child as she gently confronts this new reality is a vital part of helping with this reconciliation need of mourning.

Remember: do not expect that the child's acknowledgment of the reality will be similar to an adult's response. Many children naturally respond to news of death with indifference or an apparent lack of feelings. This is the child's natural way of protecting himself; he will embrace the full reality of the death only intermittently, in doses. A lack of outward mourning does not mean that children are not moving toward the reality—they are just doing it in their own way and time.

The ability to acknowledge the reality of the death only comes about after the child is provided with opportunities to talk-out, play-out and even act-out the circumstances of the death. Typically, the child does not embrace the full sense of loss until several months after the death. (Meeting this need can take years if the child has been told half-truths or even out-and-out lied to about the reality of the death.) Prior to that, the child will likely, consciously and unconsciously, work to distance himself from the pain that is part and parcel of meeting this critical first mourning need.

For the adult caregiver, the art of helping meet this need lies in balancing the child's need to acknowledge this new reality with the child's normal desire to push the reality away.

Need 2. Move toward the pain of the loss while being nurtured physically, emotionally, and spiritually.

To heal, the grieving child must not just be allowed but encouraged to embrace the wide range of thoughts and feelings that result from the death.

This task is often complicated by adults who want to protect the child from the impact of the death. This tendency is understandable, but in prematurely moving the child away from the hurts of grief, well-intentioned but misinformed adults can interfere with the child's healing and may even cause long-term harm.

The desire of many adults to "spare children" is often caused by their own feelings of discomfort, fear, or anxiety. The reasoning? If adults can get the child to avoid feelings of pain and hurt, they won't have to "be with" the child in the grief journey. The sad reality is that many adults will try to protect themselves from pain by protecting children from pain.

On the other hand, we must be careful not to blame or shame those adults who have adopted this overprotective stance. After all, we have all grown up in a culture in which the role of pain is misunderstood. In our society, to feel and express thoughts and feelings (or in a child's situation, to play or act out these feelings) connected to loss is often considered unnecessary and inappropriate. Mourning makes us uncomfortable. Yet, in reality, it is in moving toward our hurts that we ultimately heal.

So, to heal from losses in our culture takes tremendous courage, particularly for children. Why? Because many children must overcome adult behaviors such as isolation, deception, and overprotection from the events surrounding death.

The art of helping grieving children with this need is to allow them to teach you how they feel. You cannot prod children into this, but you can work to create a safe, nurturing environment where they sense your desire to understand.

Grieving children need permission to mourn. Sometimes what they need most from adults is an awareness that it is OK to talk out and play out their many thoughts and feelings. If the suffering is avoided, denied, or repressed by adults surrounding grieving children, those very children will be abandoned at a time when they most need the presence of loving adults. Actually, it's not really a question of, "Will the child feel or not feel?" It is a question of, "When he feels, will he be able to express himself in the companionship of loving adults?"

Note, too, that moving toward the pain of the loss is just one facet of this reconciliation need. The child's simultaneous need to be nurtured physically, emotionally and spiritually is the other facet. Physically, the child needs adequate nutrition and hydration, daily rest, and regular physical activity. Her emotional needs are many, but at bottom what she needs is a safe psychological environment and a nurturing support system that assures her she is loved and cared for. And the grieving child's spiritual needs include such things as embracing "meaning of life" issues in the face of death.

Need 3. Convert the relationship with the person who has died from one of presence to one of memory.

This reconciliation need involves allowing and encouraging the child to move from the "here and now" of his relationship with the person who died to the "what was." Though the grieving child should not be expected to give up all ties to the person who died (actually it is unwise and often damaging to communicate to the child that any and all relationships with the person who died are over), there must be an alteration of the relationship from one of presence to one of memory.

Precious memories, occasional dreams reflecting the significance of the relationship, and living legacies are among the manifestations of this different form of a continued relationship. The process of beginning to embrace memories often begins with the funeral. Unfortunately, there are some adults who prevent children from this vital part of the work of mourning by excluding them from the funeral. Remembering the person who has died through the funeral helps affirm the value of the life that was lived.

In fact, the memories that families share during this time often set the tone for the changed nature of the relationship. The ritual encourages the expression of cherished memories and allows for both tears and laughter. Memories that were made in love can be gently embraced in the companionship of loving adults.

Remembering can be a very slow, painful, and incremental process. When children are particularly hurting from the sting of grief, nonjudgmental support and understanding may be what is most needed. However, sometimes as caring adults we must encourage the gentle encountering of memories. Stimulating the child to keep memories alive rather than blocking them out helps affirm the value of the relationship. In a culture where many people do not understand the value and function of memories, most grieving children will need help meeting this important mourning need. There are many ways you can help grieving children with memory work. A few examples are noted below:

• Modeling the expressions of your own feelings and memories.
• Encouraging the child to teach you about some of her own memories.
• Providing the child with keepsakes that belonged to the person who died.

- Allowing the child to be involved in the funeral ritual.
- Talking about experiences the child had with the person who died.
- Displaying photos of the person who died.
- Visiting places of special significance that stimulate memories.
- Naturally bringing up the person who died in conversations with the child.
- Reviewing photo albums together at special times like holidays, birthdays, and anniversaries.
- Keeping in mind any major milestones that might create occasions for reminiscing, e.g. graduating from grade school to middle school, the child's own birthday, etc.

Perhaps one of the best ways to embrace memories is through the creation of a "Memory Book"—a scrapbook containing photos, mementos, letters, reflective writings, etc. that commemorate the person who died. This scrapbook will often become a valued collection of memories that the child will call upon often during her grief journey.

Special mention should be made of children with ambivalent memories, particularly those children whose memories are marked by emotional, physical, or sexual abuse. These kinds of experiences make it naturally difficult to openly embrace memories. These children need nonjudgmental adults they trust enough to explore these painful memories with. Obviously, these kinds of memories complicate the task of mourning and require your special attention. Children who are not helped to place these memories in perspective (and helped to understand that they were victims) may carry an underlying sadness or anger into their adult lives.

My experience in learning from thousands of grieving children is that remembering makes hoping possible. Grieving children's futures become open to new experiences and relationships to the extent that past memories have been embraced.

Need 4. Develop a new self-identity based on a life without the person who died.

Among the most difficult changes the grieving child encounters are those that reflect his or her personal identity. Personal identity or self-perception comes from the ongoing process of establishing a sense of who one is. The death of someone loved can, and often does, permanently change the child's self-perception.

To experience the death of a parent, grandparent, brother or sister, or best friend is among life's most stressful encounters for children. The specific roles the person who has died played in the child's life are critical to the child's self-definition. As ten-year-old Katie said after the death of her mother, "I used to have a mommy who loved me and took care of me. Now I don't have a mommy here for me anymore."

Obviously Katie was confronted with the difficult task of redefining herself without the presence of her loving mother.

Social and functional role changes must be integrated into the grieving child's new identity. For example, having a mother or father is typically a vital part of a child's self-concept. To go from having a mother or father to not having one is a process, not an event. Beyond the change in self-identity, there is also the loss of the "old" part of one's self—the significant part attached to one's parent. The child is mourning the loss not only on the outside, but also on the inside.

The grieving child's identity is also impacted in that she becomes aware that she and others around her are mortal. She learns that she is not immune from the potential of experiencing losses in life. Some of these children develop a more serious or cautious view of themselves that reflects this sense of vulnerability. As caring adults, we must be watchful that this potential seriousness does not hinder the child's long-term capacity to play and have fun. Sometimes grieving children who haven't been helped to work through such feelings grow to become chronically depressed adults. This is a reminder that working with grieving children is an excellent way of practicing preventive, proactive mental health care.

On the brighter side, I have also seen many grieving children evolve more compassionate self-identities. They often develop a special sensitivity to the needs of others, demonstrate patience, and have a gift for being nurturing. Essentially, their experience of personal suffering can enhance their ability to be sensitive, compassionate and aware of the needs of others who have losses in life. A way I like to say it is that the grieving child's gift in helping others often comes from embracing and learning from the pain of his own loss.

Need 5. Relate the experience of the death to a context of meaning.

This reconciliation need involves allowing the child to search for and restore a sense of meaning in life after the death. After the death of someone loved, the child's perception of the meaning and purpose of life is naturally changed. Many adults are surprised to learn that even young children search for meaning when they are grieving.

In the process of working on this reconciliation need of mourning, meaning is usually searched for through "How?" and "Why?" questions. The grieving child will only verbalize these to adults whom he trusts. When these conditions are met, the child will teach you about his search for meaning not only in words, but more frequently through play and acting-out behaviors.

A few examples of questions the child might naturally be exploring are: "How could a drunk driver crash and kill my mommy?"; "Why didn't my daddy's body work right?"; and "How can my sister die when she is younger than me?"

It is interesting to note that many adults make the mistake of thinking they must always have answers to the grieving child's cosmic questions. An essential component of truly helping grieving children is to know we don't have all the answers. In acknowledging our "not knowing," we ultimately become more helpful to the child who is searching for meaning. This may seem paradoxical, yet it appears to hold true in my work with thousands of grieving children.

Inherent to the child's work on this reconciliation need is suffering. As caring adults, we naturally feel uncomfortable when we see a child who is hurting physically, emotionally, or spiritually. Yet, suffering is a painful yet natural part of the work of mourning.

I would be remiss here if I did not note that the many children subject to great hunger, poverty and deprivation are not experiencing growth through such suffering. As a matter of fact, premature death is usually the consequence of this kind of suffering. This teaches us that basic security needs must be fulfilled before a grieving child can do work related to the search for meaning.

However, when these basic needs are met, hundreds of grieving children have helped me understand that they can and do respond to the death with an amazing capacity to search for and find continued meaning in their lives:

Six-year-old Charles taught me, "Ghosts have learned goodness from the people in my life that have died."

Eight-year-old Diane taught me, "The people in Heaven have my grandma to watch over them now."

Ten-year-old James taught me, "When I feel sad I think of all the fun times we had."

Sixteen-year-old Shawn taught me, "Since my mom's death I'm very aware of other teenagers who I can help with their losses."

With support and understanding, grieving children usually learn early in life that human beings cannot have complete control over themselves and their world. They learn that faith and hope are central to finding meaning in whatever one does in this short life. They learn a true appreciation for life and what it has to offer. They learn that it's the little things that sometimes matter the most. They learn a growing sense of gratefulness for all that life has to offer. They learn to look for the goodness in others. They learn an empathetic appreciation for the suffering of others. And, perhaps most of all, they learn to meet not only their own needs, but how to help others meet theirs.

Need 6. Experience a continued supportive adult presence in future years.

We have come to understand that grief is a process, not an event. The long-term nature of grief means that bereaved children will need adult "stabilizers" in their lives long after the event of the death. Unfortunately, because our society places so much value on the ability to "carry on," "keep your chin up" and "keep busy," many grieving children are abandoned shortly after the event of the death.

In spite of our awareness that children mourn long after the death occurs, attitudes are slow to change. "It will be best not to talk about it," "It's over and done with" and "It's time to get on with life" still dominate the messages that many grieving children are greeted with. Obviously, these kinds of messages inhibit grief rather than allow for its expression. Those persons who see children's grief as something that must be overcome or simply endured typically do not remain available to the child very long after the event of the death. In my observation, these adults encourage children to go around their grief, instead of toward or through it.

Even those children who actively participate in the work of mourning will need stabilizing adults in their lives long after the event of the death. As the child grows into adulthood, she will mourn the loss in different ways at various developmental phases.

To be truly helpful, adult caregivers must appreciate the impact of loss on children. They must understand that to heal, the child must be allowed and encouraged to mourn long after the event of the death. They must view grief not as an enemy to be overcome, but as a necessary consequence of having loved.

The "bereaved" label is an attempt on the part of society to identify a group of people with special needs. The bereaved child does have special needs. One of the most important is the need to be companioned long after the event of the death. As caring adults, we have a responsibility to remain available to these children long into the future.

I hope this discussion of the Reconciliation Needs of Mourning will help you help the grieving children in your life. Each of the six reconciliation needs I have outlined is accompanied by its own challenges and stresses to both the child and the helper. Thank you for your commitment to helping grieving children.

Guidelines for Involving Children in the Funeral

Although children may not completely understand the ceremony surrounding the death, adults need to involve them in the experience of the funeral. This involvement helps establish a sense of comfort and the understanding that life goes on even though someone they love has died.

Since the funeral is a significant event, children should have the same opportunity to attend as any other member of the family. They should be allowed to attend, never forced. Parents should explain the purpose of the funeral. It's an opportunity to help, support, and comfort each other, as well as a time to honor the life of the person who has died.

Funerals provide a unique opportunity for the natural expression of grief and allow those attending to say "thank you" for the privilege of knowing and caring for the person who has died. Most importantly, funerals are also a means of affirming that life goes on even though it is significantly different from when the person loved was alive.

Parents need to keep in mind the following factors regarding children and funerals:

- While they should be encouraged to attend the funeral, children must feel they have been given a genuine choice.
- Children need to know ahead of time what they will see and experience at the funeral (flowers, who will be coming, and how long the funeral will last).
- Children also need to know that the people they will see at the funeral will probably be expressing a wide variety of emotions. They need to know it's natural to cry.
- Children's first visits to the funeral home should be with only a few people who are especially close to them. This allows children more freedom to react and talk openly about feelings and concerns.
- Before, during and after the funeral, children need the physical closeness and comfort of parents and other caring adults. Specific words may not be as important as a hug or a hand to hold.
- Adults should anticipate that children may show little, if any, outward sign of grief at the funeral. This apparent lack of externalized mourning does not mean that children are not affected by the death.
- At the funeral, children will be teaching what the death means to them.
- Adults need to be good observers of children's behavior at the funeral and realize that being patient and empathetic is important at this time.

Additional Helping Guidelines for Caring Adults

Be good observers. Don't rush in with ready explanations. It's often more helpful to ask exploring questions than to give quick answers.

- When describing the death of a loved one, use simple and direct language.
- Be honest. Express personal feelings about the death. When you do so, children have a model for expressing their own feelings.
- Allow children to express a full range of feelings. Anger, guilt, despair and protest are natural reactions to the death of a loved one.
- Listen to children; don't just talk to them.
- Don't expect children's reactions to be obvious and immediate at the time of the death. Be patient and available.
- Recognize that no one procedure or formula will fit all children, either at the time of the death or during the months that follow. Be patient, flexible, and adjust to individual needs.
- Adults must explore their own personal feelings about death. Until they consciously examine their own concerns, doubts and fears about death, it will be difficult to support children when someone loved has died.

Adolescent Mourning: A Naturally Complicated Experience

Each year, thousands of teenagers experience the death of someone they love. As adults do, these survivors grieve (the internal experiencing of thoughts and feelings following a death) but often do not mourn (the external, shared social response to the loss). Unfortunately, adolescents hear messages from well-intentioned adults such as "Keep your chin up," "Keep busy," or "Carry on."

Steve, age 18, is a good example of a grieving teenager who was denied the right to mourn the death of his mother. Finally, three years after her death, he was able to talk openly about the experience. Steve said, "When my mom died, I thought my heart would break, but I couldn't cry." Friends and family told Steve to "be strong" and that he "could take it." For Steve, the result of repressing his grief was a feeling of anger, sadness and isolation.

Obviously, these messages advocating denial prevent Steve or any adolescent from doing the work of mourning. In addition, a number of other factors often make mourning during this period in a teenager's life a naturally complicated experience. These factors include concurrent developmental tasks; sudden, often premature deaths; unique environmental conditions; and the potential of conflicting relationships.

Concurrent Developmental Tasks

With the exception of infancy, no developmental period is as filled with changes as adolescence. Consequently, the death of a parent, sibling, relative or friend can be devastating during this already developmentally difficult time. At the time the grieving adolescent is facing the death, he or she is often experiencing significant psychological, physiological and academic pressures.

Psychologically, one of the most difficult but necessary tasks for a teenager is to leave the security of childhood and begin the process of separation from parents. The paradox is, however, that as adolescents strive for independence, they are still dependent on their families for most psychological and physical needs. The death of a family member naturally threatens the maintenance of these needs.

Because adolescence is often accompanied by awkward physical development, teenagers sometimes feel unattractive. This difficulty with physical self-acceptance makes it hard to have consistently positive self-esteem and affects how teenagers respond to the death of a loved one. Adults need to remember that physical development does not always include emotional maturity. While teenagers may begin to look like adults, they still need consistent and compassionate support—just like children—while they are mourning.

Academic achievement and competition are also complicating factors in grieving teenagers' worlds. While they are trying to survive the death of someone in their lives, pressure often exists to go to college and even get into the "right college." Struggling with a loss sometimes makes it difficult for them to perceive the value that adults are placing on academics and higher education.

During adolescence, teenagers have a tremendous amount of growing up to do—physically and emotionally. These concurrent developmental tasks make it hard for them to mourn in constructive, healthy ways. Adults need to be aware of these accompanying tasks and encourage bereaved teens to teach them about grief.

Sudden, Often Premature Deaths

Many of the deaths that touch the lives of adolescents are unexpected and traumatic. A parent dies of a sudden heart attack. A brother or sister is killed in an automobile accident. Or a friend commits suicide. The very nature of these kinds of deaths often results in a prolonged and heightened sense of unreality for teenagers.

The traumatic nature of these deaths is compounded by the very intense relationships teenagers often have with the people in their lives. Family break-ups often result in teenagers living with grandparents. Even if warning precedes the grandparent's death, the loss is significant and painful.

Most adolescents also have intense relationships with their siblings. There is often competition, rivalry, and components of both love and hate. Should a brother or sister die suddenly, a natural sense of blame or responsibility can occur. Teens also can be extremely close to friends. As when a sibling dies, teenagers need an opportunity to mourn the death of a best friend.

Traumatic deaths make the grief work for teenagers complicated. They sometimes find it difficult to accept the intensity of the painful feelings of grief that they are experiencing. And, as a result of growing feelings of independence, teenagers don't want to accept adult help in coping with these feelings. Yet as with children, adult support and understanding during this time is critical.

Unique Environmental Conditions

Adults assume that when a death occurs, adolescents are surrounded by supportive family and friends. In reality, this situation may not be true at all. The lack of available support often makes adults place inappropriate social expectations on grieving teens. Teenager, for example, are expected to be grown-up and responsible for caring for others in the family, particularly a surviving parent or younger brothers and sisters. When this occurs, teenagers do not give themselves permission to mourn, nor are they given permission by others.

While regressive behavior is a normal response to the death, sometimes adolescents are openly encouraged to be hypermature and accept responsibility far beyond their years. Like children, teenagers fall into the "Big-Man" and "Big-Woman" syndrome. The result is a repression of mourning for the adolescent and the possibility of a delayed grief response later in life.

Another unique environmental condition experienced by grieving adolescents involves the changing nature of family life today. Historically, the extended family offered understanding during times of distress. The teenager could turn to aunts or uncles for support.

Today, however, Americans often live far away from their extended family. We also tend to relocate frequently. This mobility makes it more difficult for families to reach out to one another for understanding. Such a fast-paced, mobile culture results in increased isolation for teenagers when someone loved dies. In addition, peers often provide little or no support to grieving teenagers. Their grief is often met with indifference, except in circumstances in which a friend has also experienced the death of a family member. More typically, however, peers choose to ignore the subject of loss entirely.

Potential of Conflicting Relationships

As teenagers move toward independence, relationship conflicts are common. A normal, although trying, way teens separate from parents is by going through a period of "devaluation." If, however, a parent dies while the teenager is pushing the parent away, the teenager often experiences a heightened sense of guilt. While the need to create this distance is healthy, it complicates the experience of mourning for adolescents.

A majority of this conflict between teenagers and parents comes from the normal process of forming independent identities and values. Death combined with the turbulence of this relationship often makes it critical for the adolescent to talk about what the relationship was like before the parent died.

Another factor that influences a teenager's complications with grief is the heightened sense of ambivalence the teen feels about his or her parents. Adolescence is sometimes commensurate with parental love-hate relationships. If the parent dies, talking about this ambivalence seems essential to doing the work of mourning. Unfortunately, many teenagers do not have such a conversation. A relationship based on trust is required.

In contrast, a teenager may have the opposite of an ambivalent relationship with a parent. Instead, the teen may be hyperdependent. This is particularly true for adolescents with poor social or communication skills who have difficulty creating and maintaining meaningful peer relationships. If the parent dies, the teenager often experiences a total sense of isolation and hopelessness.

Conflicting relationships for teenagers also occur with boyfriends and girlfriends. If a conflict is in progress when the death occurs, the adolescent may be left with a feeling of unfinished business. Or the teen may feel guilty for the death. In such circumstances, these teenagers can be at risk for suicide and, as a result, require special attention.

Consequences of Postponed Mourning in the Adolescent

The specific reasons grieving adolescents have difficulty with mourning in healthy ways are multiple and complicated. Major roadblocks stand in their way. The most common consequences of this complicated grief process among teenagers are:

- Symptoms of chronic depression, sleeping difficulties, restlessness and low-esteem.
- Academic failure or general indifference to school-related activities.
- Deterioration in relationships with family and friends, often leading to trouble forming intimate relationships in adulthood.
- Acting out in a variety of ways: drug and alcohol abuse, fighting and inappropriate risk-taking, and sexual behavior.

- Denial of grief with an accompanying demonstration of hypermaturity.
- Symptoms of chronic anxiety and agitation.

A Final Note About Adolescent Mourning

Caring adults must be especially supportive and understanding of grieving teens. Experiencing the death of a loved one is never easy, no matter what the age of the survivor. But the adolescent years hold a particular challenge and require a concerted effort by adults to help the teenager do the work of mourning.

Final Thoughts About Children and Grief

For children, the journey through grief is complex. And each child's journey is unique. Caring adults need to communicate to children that these feelings are not something to be ashamed of or to hide. Instead, grief is a natural expression of love for the person who has died.

For caring adults, the challenge is clear: children do not choose between grieving and not grieving. Adults, on the other hand, do have a choice—to help or not to help children cope with grief.

As demonstrated by reading this book, your choice is obviously to help. Congratulations on expanding your knowledge of this important subject. I hope this experience will be just a beginning, and you will continue to build your awareness through additional grief education. Inspire others to do the same.

With education, plus love and understanding, "helping-healing" adults can guide children through this vulnerable time and make it a valuable part of children's personal growth and development.

My Grief Rights
A Bill of Rights for Grieving Kids

1. I have the right to have my own unique feelings about the death. I might feel mad, sad or lonely. I might feel scared or relieved. I might feel numb or sometimes not anything at all. No one will feel exactly like I do.

2. I have the right to talk about my grief whenever I feel like talking. When I need to talk, I will find someone who will listen to me and love me. When I don't want to talk, that's OK, too.

3. I have the right to show my feelings of grief in my own way. When they are hurting, some kids like to play so they'll feel better for awhile. I can play or laugh, too. I might also get mad and misbehave. This does not mean I am bad, it just means I have scary feelings that I need help with.

4. I have the right to need other people to help me with my grief, especially grown-ups who care about me. Mostly I need them to pay attention to what I am feeling and saying and to love me no matter what.

5. I have the right to get upset about normal, everyday problems. I might feel grumpy and have trouble getting along with others sometimes.

6. I have the right to have "griefbursts." Griefbursts are sudden, unexpected feelings of sadness that just hit me sometimes—even long after the death. These feelings can be very strong and even scary. When this happens, I might feel afraid to be alone.

7. I have the right to use my beliefs about God to help me with my grief. Praying might make me feel better and somehow closer to the person who died.

8. I have the right to try to figure out why the person I loved died. But it's OK if I don't find an answer. Why questions about life and death are the hardest questions in the world.

9. I have the right to think and talk about my memories of the person who died. Sometimes those memories will be happy and sometimes they might be sad. Either way, memories help me keep alive my love for the person who died.

10. I have the right to move toward and feel my grief and, over time, to heal. I'll go on to live a happy life, but the life and death of the person who died will always be a part of me. I'll always miss the person who died.

My Grief Rights is available as a full-color poster from Companion Press. To order, call (970) 226-6050 or visit www.centerforloss.com. Wallet card versions are also available.

ALSO BY ALAN WOLFELT

Healing A Child's Grieving Heart:
100 Practical Ideas for Families, Friends and Caregivers

Healing A Child's Grieving Heart is for families, friends and caregivers who want practical, day-to-day tips for helping the grieving children they love. Some of the ideas teach about children's unique mourning styles and needs. Others suggest simple activities and "companioning" tips. A compassionate, easy-to-read resource for parents, aunts and uncles, grandparents, teachers, volunteers—and a great refresher for professional caregivers.

ISBN 1-879651-28-9 • 128 pages • softcover • $11.95

Healing Your Grieving Heart for Kids:
100 Practical Ideas

Healing Your Grieving Heart for Kids is for young and middle readers (6-12 year-olds) grieving the death of someone loved. The text is simple and straightforward, teaching children about grief and affirming that their thoughts and feelings are not only normal but necessary. Page after page of age-appropriate activities and gentle, healing guidance.

ISBN 1-879651-27-0 • 128 pages • softcover • $11.95

ALSO BY ALAN WOLFELT

Healing the Bereaved Child:
Grief Gardening, Growth Through Grief and Other Touchstones for Caregivers

One spring morning a gardener noticed an unfamiliar seedling poking through the ground near the rocky, untended edge of his garden . . .

So begins the parable that sets the tone for this inspiring, heartfelt classic for caregivers to bereaved children. By comparing grief counseling to gardening, Dr. Wolfelt frees caregivers of the traditional medical model of bereavement care, which implies that grief is an illness that must be cured. He suggests that caregivers instead embrace a more holistic view of the normal, natural and necessary process that is grief. He then explores the ways in which bereaved children can not only heal but grow through grief.

Illustrated throughout with specially commissioned photos of children by fine art photographer Patrick Dean, *Healing the Bereaved Child* also contains chapter after chapter of practical caregiving guidelines:

• My Guiding Model: Growth-oriented Grief Gardening with Bereaved Children
• Mourning Styles: What Makes Each Child's Grief Unique
• Sad/Scared/Mad/Tired/Glad: How a Grieving Child Thinks, Feels and Mourns
• How the Bereaved Child Heals: The Six Reconciliation Needs of Mourning
• Grief Gardening Basics: Foundations of Counseling Bereaved Children
• The Grief Gardener's Tools: Techniques for Counseling Bereaved Children
• Grief Gardening and the Family: A Systems Approach to Healing the Bereaved Child
• The "Cold Frames" of Grief Gardening: Support Groups for Bereaved Children
• The Child's Garden: Helping Grieving Children at School
• Grief Gardening in June: The Grieving Adolescent
• The Grief Gardener's Gazebo: The Importance of Self-Care

Part textbook, part workbook, part meditation, this exhilarating guide is a must-read for child counselors, hospice caregivers, funeral directors, school counselors and teachers, clergy, parents—anyone who wants to offer support and companionship to children affected by the death of someone loved.

ISBN 1-879651-10-6
8 1/2" x 11" format • 344 pages • softcover • $39.95

ALSO BY ALAN WOLFELT

Healing A Teen's Grieving Heart:
100 Practical Ideas for Families, Friends & Caregivers

Healing A Teen's Grieving Heart: 100 Practical Ideas for Families, Friends and Caregivers is for adults who want practical, day-to-day "how-tos" for helping the grieving teens in their lives. Some of the ideas teach about teenagers' unique mourning styles and needs—which are particularly complicated because of the teen's already difficult developmental tasks. Other ideas suggest simple activities and tips for relating to and spending time with the grieving teen.

ISBN 1-879651-24-6 • 128 pages • softcover • $11.95

Healing Your Grieving Heart for Teens:
100 Practical Ideas

In this compassionate book for grieving teenagers, Dr. Wolfelt speaks honestly and straightforwardly to teens, affirming their thoughts and feelings and giving them dozens of teen-friendly ideas for understanding and coping with their grief. The book also acknowledges teenagers' natural tendencies to spurn adult help while encouraging them to express their grief. Unlike longer, more text-dense books on grief, the one-idea-per-page format is inviting and readable for this age group.

ISBN 1-879651-23-8 • 128 pages • softcover • $11.95

ALSO BY ALAN WOLFELT

The Healing Your Grieving Heart Journal for Teens
With a foreword by Brian Griese

Teenagers often don't want to talk to adults—or even to their friends—about their struggles. But given the opportunity, many will choose the more private option of writing. Many grieving teens find that journaling helps them sort through their confusing thoughts and feelings.

Yet few journals created just for teens exist and even fewer address the unique needs of the grieving teen. In the Introduction, this unique journal—written by Dr. Wolfelt and his 14-year-old daughter, Megan—affirms the grieving teen's thoughts and feelings and offers gentle, healing guidance. The six central needs of mourning are explained, as are common grief responses. Throughout, the authors provide simple, open-ended questions for the grieving teen to explore, such as:

- What do you miss most about the person who died?
- Write down one special memory.
- Which feelings have been most difficult for you since the death? Why?
- Is there something you wish you had said to the person who died but never did?
- Describe the personality of the person who died. Tape a photo here, too, if you'd like.

Designed just for grieving teens as a companion to Dr. Wolfelt's bestselling *Healing Your Grieving Heart for Teens: 100 Practical Ideas*, this journal will be a comforting, affirming and healing presence for teens in the weeks, months and years after the death of someone loved.

ISBN 1-879651-33-5 • 128 pages • softcover • $11.95